MEDITATION ON A TOOTH

ESSENTIAL POETS SERIES 316

Canada Council for the Arts
Conseil des Arts du Canada

ONTARIO ARTS COUNCIL
CONSEIL DES ARTS DE L'ONTARIO
an Ontario government agency
un organisme du gouvernement de l'Ont

Ontario

Canada

Guernica Editions Inc. acknowledges the support of the Canada Council for the Arts and the Ontario Arts Council. The Ontario Arts Council is an agency of the Government of Ontario.

We acknowledge the financial support of the Government of Canada.

KENNETH SHERMAN

MEDITATION ON A TOOTH

Poems

GUERNICA EDITIONS

TORONTO – BUFFALO – LANCASTER (U.K.)

2025

Guernica Founder: Antonio D'Alfonso

Michael Mirolla, editor
Cover and interior design: Errol F. Richardson

Guernica Editions Inc.
1241 Marble Rock Rd., Gananoque, (ON), Canada K7G 2V4
2250 Military Road, Tonawanda, N.Y. 14150-6000 U.S.A.
www.guernicaeditions.com

Distributors:
University of Toronto Press Distribution (UTP)
5201 Dufferin Street, Toronto (ON), Canada M3H 5T8
Independent Publishers Group (IPG)
814 N Franklin Street, Chicago, IL 60610, U.S.A.

First edition.
Printed in Canada.

Legal Deposit – First Quarter
Library of Congress Catalogue Card Number: 2024945645
Library and Archives Canada Cataloguing in Publication
Title: Meditation on a tooth : poems / Kenneth Sherman.
Other titles: Meditation on a tooth (Compilation)
Names: Sherman, Kenneth, 1950- author.
Series: Essential poets ; 316.
Description: Series statement: Essential poets series ; 316
Identifiers: Canadiana 2024045491X | ISBN 9781771839587
(softcover)
Subjects: LCGFT: Poetry.
Classification: LCC PS8587.H3863 M43 2025 | DDC
C811/.54—dc23

Contents

III

For Aiden, Jacob, and Mia

I

Spy Balloon

You can picture it
sluggish, white
floating over airfields and silos
collecting data
with a face serene as the Buddha's

or maybe with a crazed smirk
like the Joker's
snooping the shadows and laneways
snapping pics of pets, plants,
bicycles, in living colour.

Of course, it has no face

nor should you confuse it
as you peer through your telescope's lens
with the moon
climbing cold and passive.

This furious memory machine
works with intermittent beeps
and ratchets
figuring the trajectories
in decimals and integers
making sure you are marked and counted
which is not the same
as chosen.
                    Chosen
means you're human.

To My Musa Basjoo Tree in Time of War

Now I can say what you mean
with your six-foot paddle-shaped leaves
offering protection from rain
and sun
                    yet easily wind-broken,
easily torn and frayed.

Still, you're a survivor
with flowers that are tubular
and scentless

fruit that's inedible

wood — unfit for any building
or making — untouched
by saw or axe.

It's your very uselessness
that ensures your existence,
making you indispensable
to me
               as I sit beneath your sagging limbs
listening to the echo of shells,
the far-off shrieks, the crackling fires
of destruction

wishing for a time
other than the time
the two of us
live in.

War Photographer

. . . and the news
Is war
As always
—George Oppen

She's in the field
taking photographs of the dead
who can't help but stare
into nowhere.

"What do you make of us," they ask
"with our frozen lips
that are runways
                    for flies,

our broken limbs
askew,
as if we had fallen
from the stars?"

She thinks they look
ridiculous,
    these contortionists in death.

Before she clicks
                    and shoots
she feels the need to re-arrange
their shattered bodies

to restore some dignity

while in the distance
the green mountains
sit silent.

Nowhere does she hear the voice of a prophet,

only a thin wind
rummaging through the grass.

How will she
capture that, how
will she find
what is missed?

Fire

Think of Prometheus,
his gift.

What have we done with it?

No use saying the world
was always on fire, it was never
like this:
            charred forests,
singed monoliths, swaths of smoke
drifting down so that you awake each day
with the taste of Apocalypse between your teeth.

And these fires cannot die, cannot
be extinguished, they've
gone underground, sizzling beneath
swamps and bogs and staunched streams,
running along roots and buried vines
like the lit lines of a detonator

heading into our future.

There we are, standing helpless
in the old house we're slow to abandon,
drawing in the smell
of burnt paper, the hiss of words
breathing their last.

Black-Backed Woodpecker

From deep inside the charred forest
you hear his *rat-a-tat-tat*.

He's probing burnt bark
for cowering white slugs and larvae.
There all that's left.

No arsonist, he's our winged
opportunist, dreaming conflagration:
smouldering limbs, scorched rocks,
steaming deer carcass.

Where have all the wildflowers gone?
Gone to ash.

Pickings are easy
when everything else is motionless,
air static.

No competition — singed branches
can't be camouflage
unless your feathers are undertaker black.

Is there rage from above?
Exhortations? Fury?

Rat-a-tat-tat.
Rat-a-tat-tat.

There's that.

The Road

"Who built this road?"
The nameless.

"Who ordered it?"
One of History's famous.

At the end of the road
a mine
with gold, tungsten, uranium.
For the nation.

They weren't fed much, these nameless builders.
In the end, they ate the barracks' pet dogs
and cats.

What is there to say about ethics
when you hear the howl of famished bears,
when arctic temperatures plummet
and human spit freezes in mid-air?

Some say stone can't forget.
They say the buried flesh
frozen beneath this road
is evidence.

But haven't you noticed
how Justice always lags?

Or is non-existent?

Anyway, how would Justice
help *them*?

Mumbai

An evening sky slashed red.
And off in the distance
black wings circling the Towers of Silence.
Here, they believe that burial contaminates earth,
cremation taints fire, while bird feeding is clean:
vultures' thick beaks and splayed feet shred flesh.
Bones shine like hieroglyphs.

All day there's traffic and smog,
bartering and bickering in the fragrant markets
where I hear the caws of caged parrots.

At night, beneath my hotel window
it's the tap and airy gulp
of goat-skin drums, the swelling songs
of street people sending off their newly dead.

The Orchard

This was years ago
in the peach orchards of Tzuba,
located in the hills outside of Jerusalem.
It was break time and we sat
on the cold, damp ground
our pails sprawled nearby
the fruit wagon half filled.

It was just before the war
that we knew was coming
and what could we do except sit
and speak softly of our fears
in the sweet-smelling orchard
that was as still as Eden
before man.

The Garden

The universe
is flying apart
at the speed of light
the waters are rising
soon the beach
will be an ocean floor
half of all known
species will perish
though which are marked
for extinction
no one can say
so much dismaying
news to take in
as I work
trimming the
yew, feeding
the viburnum, the
flower bed needs
weeding and I kneel
with trowel
smell the pungent earth
as the glow of
yellow petals
spreads
across my face
how can anyone
accept
that this
might end
that we will
be left on a
flooded rock
hurtling through

space, am I right
to tend my garden,
maybe I should be
holding a placard
linked arm in arm
with others, something
I am not, by nature,
inclined to do,
besides,
the poem needs
my attention
as much as the
garden,
to counter oblivion
to lower
by one decibel
the clamour.
I wish
the marchers well.

Meditation on a Tooth

1

My tooth is gone

the enamel the pulp
the nerve and dentine

little niblet of ivory

white plank
torn from my mouth's picket fence

And now that it is gone
and my tongue worms
through the shocking socket
digesting the nuance of space

I contemplate sharpness
                                        and absence

being
        and nothingness —

                                        toothfulness
and the abyss.

That tooth
was not chipped or cracked
never even filled

its light suddenly vanished
like knocked-out neon

then yanked
leaving a hole
tender to the touch
and sweet with blood
but bitter
with the awareness of age

and my departure
from this loving star

2

It was pulled by my cousin,
Dr. Larry Grossman.

He left me waiting
as the freezing set in.
I perused the dental catalogue
he'd left on the cold
metal tray

thumbnails
of cheek retractors

chisels and gouges and clamps

bone files and scalers

soldering tweezers and excavators

wax knives and explorers

root elevators and —
of course —

holloware.

“Only a tooth,” said Larry
returning
pliers in hand.
“Not a limb or eye.
Replaceable.”

The cost
                to be determined.

3

I remember him age nine
sprawled on our living room floor
disassembling our stalled antique clock
examining up-close the delicate intricacy
of gears

then carefully
reassembling

a child and already
proficient with his hands

ginger-haired metaphysician
questioning Time

grown into a suburban
dentist —
                    the evaporation
of dreams?

But isn't maintenance of molars
and incisors
essential for grinding
everyday facts
so that we have the courage to swallow
digest and endure?

4

That tooth was a barrier
against loss
                    nothing now
to prevent the toothless of my youth
from rising up with their
sink-hole grins:

Gabby Hayes

the goalies Sawchuck
            Bower
            Worsley

my grandmother in her nightie
dentures drowned
in a tumbler of water

and homeless Wild Bill
thin denizen of College Street

(my father gave him odd jobs
let him bunk winter nights
with the cats
on the cutting table of
his tailor shop
blanketed under warm yards
of English cloth.)

5

Franz Kafka
kept two of his milk teeth
in a small Chinese box

feared the open mouths
of adults — their teeth flecked
with particles of meat —
a world overrun
with *Menschen Fressers*

he suffered from troubled lungs
as well as from *Gewissensbisse* —
the bite
of conscience.

He knew that a trip to the dentist
is never mere maintenance

it is a reckoning
with poor flesh

an existential crisis
trembling with memory.

6

For how many know
that our teeth originate in stars
that eons back swelled
and broke apart violently
the finer matter sifting
through space
mixing with the thicker elements
that shape this rocky
mineral planet:

potassium for brains
calcium for teeth
iron to colour our blood
a river of red?

When we tilt our heads
and peer into the night sky
we should not think "alien"
we should not whisper "distant light"

we should sense
the radiant
continuum.

7

Francis Bacon viewed the oral cavity
as a galaxy of hard stars
glistening spittle
rich vermillion against satin black

he said he wanted to paint the mouth
"the way Monet painted
a sunset"

but ended up painting mouths
filled with screams and teeth

his Pope Innocent
seated in what looks like
an electric chair
                                        or a dentist's chair

the eyes and mouth of a hysterical horse.

8

And I consider
how my Jew-tooth
would be of zero use
to the SS
hunting gold
in the jaws of the dead

it would survive as a
testament

not dissolving
in the hastily erected
pyres of Treblinka

not hidden
in the camp's covered pit

but rising slowly
to the earth's surface
together with bone fragments
strands of black and golden hair,

shreds of singed shirts
and pants

a grim collage

to be discovered
by the journalist Vasily Grossman
(no relation to my cousin)
travelling with the Red Army
in August of 1944.

The skulls keep silent
but the sockets speak.

9

Larry has finished the twisting
and pulling

advises Tylenol
gentle brushing
salt-water rinse

measures the gap
for implant

and I am grateful
for the science of titanium
and gums

I am thankful for the technology
of porcelain and paint

the spare parts theory
of modernity.

For my tooth is truly gone —

not flying
                    to Jerusalem

not mourned
                         in any liturgy

not important enough
to be preserved like Buddha's
in the Tooth Temple
in the city of Kandy

just a common biter
put out with the clinic's waste
for environmental
disposal.

Not rising bright.

Not
starlight.

II

Dogs Listening

The dogs love music.
Look at them sitting there,
eyes bewitched,
listening to my guitar.

They have forgotten the sound of things running.
They have given up the chase.
The music has overcome them
as it has almost overcome me,
the maker of music.

Light is waning
and I bring the chords
an octave lower.

Now the dogs are lost to a rhythm,
a pulse other than their own
and they devour it, without teeth
or star-lit saliva, without black rubbery gums
or long glossy tongues.

They trot over fields
from their very first days.
Before the chase.

What, you may ask, am I doing,
reminding them of irreplaceable orchards,
clover, black fragrant earth
they can never re-visit?

Shameful, the power of art,
shameful, these notes
aimed at a poor dog's
heart,
            still, I play on
for what else will raise a dog
beyond the bone and frantic dig?

What else can I do
with these restless fingers
and hands?

Sound Check

He's seated by the mic
seemingly harmless in his
shorts and sandals
playing a few phrases
on his flamenco guitar
as the sound engineers listen in.

I'm glad I won't be here
some hours from now
when he returns
dressed in black
stage-light flashing
off his oval glasses.

I wouldn't want to hear the way
he forces his six innocent
strings to sound like
a sobbing woman or like
the wind chasing itself
through an orchard of dying trees.

White Out

Sometimes, the snow gets intense.
I know there are those who walk into it,
blinded for a moment before coming out the other end.
They dust the snow off their shoulders
and move on
                    while there are those, like you and me,
who get stuck wandering through a desert of white glare,
flakes clotting our eyelashes, the cold burning our cheeks.
Afterwards, we like to gather and talk about how low
the temperature was, how privileged we were to feel the wind
cut through our jackets. We enjoy describing the sound of its rage,
recounting the sensation of our throats freezing up,
our very words
                    gasping for breath.

Basho Says

travel light
with nothing
but a raincoat
and medicine
brushes and ink
paper and bowl
that way you will
have a chance
to travel light
into the future
with poems that use
the shortest number
of syllables

when they ask
what binds you to the rock
the pond the tree
answer with words
that are clear
as stream water
sitting in a cup
of fired clay

dust of the road
solitary starling
remember
the you that sets out
on this journey
is and is not
the you who comes back
to say what there was
before there was
anything

Watching the Sea

Wherever you lead
I have been there
beyond the salt, the storms,
the shipwreck,
                    knowing
the loneliness of your hues
that shift with the waning day

Your horizon is only
part of it, there are
your corals, your depths
your plastics,

are you tired of buoying tankers, freighters,
aircraft carriers

the cruise ships with their filled
freezers, their tables

of roulette

are you tired
dispelling the tedium
of those who must stay
in motion

today you look calm and ancient
ennobled
by the words I arrive at
without ever having left

To an Old Building

You inhabit me
as much as I
inhabit you

the storm surges
and the summer heat
baked into your roof
and walls

the salt and sand
etched
into your concrete columns

your worn windows
staring out at the sea

what is that low persistent hum
that runs through the hallways
and the lobby
and through each apartment
like the soundtrack
from *Eraserhead*

or like the wind I heard
chasing itself
in the burial cave
outside of Akko
where the archaeologist
showed me the pottery shards
and sandal straps
but no bones

the bones
had been devoured
by the years
the things owned
lasting longer
than their owner

as you will last longer
than me

longer than
my memory

is that what your hum
is saying

your windows
looking out and in

To New Year's Day

The gulls veer off
knowing how to fly as one
leaving me alone
to watch you flush red
with dawn's anticipation
then slowly soften into blue

why do you always
turn out the same
your clouds building and sailing
as they always have
your bright light
gradually dissipating
turning ashen
before dwindling down
into a darkness
that is mine
to work through

The Light

Now that vacancy and loss widen
I feel the temptation to follow you
to join you and keep you company
though you are beyond company
without sight or touch or hearing
not even recognizable as stone or ash
but fading into a light I sometimes sense
and search for when everything else fails
when even these words fail
and the emptiness that is you
comes finally to inhabit me
and the light settles in.

Winter Garden

They're down there:
roots, bulbs, tubers,
ducking the icy air
keeping a low profile
holding firm against
what's cold and despotic.
You know what it's like
to grip darkness, to follow
an underground strategy,
a downward holding of days
until time begins to widen
with increments of light.
Up above, dry stalks of
hydrangea, split branches,
spruce needles and
spikes of the straggly yew
huddled by this rotting post,
this rusted fragment of fence.
What makes waiting bearable
is the expectation of fuchsia,
crocus, baby's breath —
living things that are transient,
tenacious.

Lazarus

After my illness
I was lifted up long enough
to gaze out my window

at the moonlit glaze of ice
on the trunk
of the Siberian elm

long enough to hear a dog
bark on a night too cold
for any living thing.

Dirt Country

I

You never notice
the golden pollen
on your work gloves,
You're busy with shovel,
hoe, stakes and string,
breaking dry earth, prepping
for beans and tomatoes,
digging and living.

II

Remember the one
who seldom spoke, the one
who fastened loose shingles,
cleaned out the hornets' nest,
mended torn screens.
One morning he just left, not bothering
to wind up the garden hose
snaking over the anemic grass.

III

Crawl under the foundation.
Beneath the damp planks and broken
bricks you'll find inchworms
and slugs — poor boy's bait.
The arthritic oars
take you far enough
to find bullet-shaped fish.
Splayed bones on your chipped plate.

IV

Whenever a breeze scours
the corn field, you hear
the dried stalks chatter. And crows
overhead, the heavy beat
of their wings. Whoever said
the country is heaven
couldn't read omens, didn't know
crows never sing.

Saint Scarecrow

Hangs there,
silent, restrained,
willing to look
the other way when
a couple of crows
land on his hat,
flap their dark wings
and start

to take him apart.

Bat

How did you enter?
A crack under the eavestrough?
An open door? And why this detour?
I thought you'd follow the night's summer swarm
back to that hollowed-out tree where you hang upside down
like a worn leather glove with the sibling hordes.
Soon I'll have you in a pickle jar with a screw-on lid.
I'll have a close-up of your snout,
your twitchy ears, your naked needle teeth.
You're ugly as sin, though sin has nothing to do with it.
You're more than a film prop, a blood drop,
a jagged shadow flicking across the moon.
You haven't bit me.
No danger here of becoming Bella Lugosi,
talking strange.

Bit Parts

1

"Travel light," grandfather instructed.
He told us there was no God,
only stationmasters.
And clocks with no hands.

2

Grandmother kept a carp in the bathtub.
It had little room to manoeuvre.
Its days were numbered.
We watched it grow inward.

3

I didn't know if I was attracted to her
or to my idea of her.
Nevertheless, her voice
chimed.

4

He calls his dog Rimbaud,
and lets him eat scraps wherever they land.
Things were not always so easy.

5

She gave me her word.
I can feel it breathing,
in my breast pocket.

6

The forests
on their knees,
begging for mercy.

7

Like an aging spider spinning his frail web
and thinking of women.
Their faint buzz.

8

Once you get seriously ill
people speak about you in whispers.
They fear you might be listening in.

9

So happy are we
beyond the reach of the ancient sea,
beyond angels and devils
and unaccountable miracles.

10

When he starts ranking his fellow poets
she reminds him: *Different birds,*
different songs.

11

Imagine a world where you can defuse
any argument by bringing up the name of a great book.
Dubliners, for example.
If that doesn't work, try *The Ambassadors*.

12

A small bus station on the outskirts of the city
growing garbage instead of flowers.
You can smell the despair.

13

He misses her. But he can't say she's like a flower or a tree.
She's too fast moving while he's rooted to his desk
fumbling with words that are determined to fall
like leaves.

14

Why do I hear the spotted trout lilies
singing like Pan's chorus
when they're just mouthfuls of silence?

15

The sad heavy animals
on ice floes
waving to us
on shore.

16

Fires, wars, mudslides, pestilence.
My granddaughter
in the shadow of the Siberian elm
singing softly
to the crickets.

Propagating Palms

Their tall trunks are phallic,
though when they sway in the wind
one thinks of tousle-haired
women. And the word, frond — fan-leaved
or feathered — is feminine.
In Latin, things go one way
or the other. The trees
are bi- or uni-sexual,
suggesting nature's somewhat
liberal, though pollen
must meet stamen
or nothing much
will happen.

"You Really Got Me"

I was full of rage. I could easily have slashed my wrists,
but I had a little green amplifier that was sounding crap.
I thought, "I'll teach it" – and slashed the speaker cone.
—Dave Davies, lead guitar, The Kinks

What's unexpected
finds its way. Consider
the kid guitarist, testy,
pissed, slashing his
amp — a little Elpico —
and presto, he's found
a new sound, throaty and
thick. Any tone
that's overdriven
gains until distortion
becomes an anthem
operating with the range
of a rusted muffler.
It carries to the ear
of a Townsend,
or a Hendrix.
It crosses
the Atlantic.

Tropics

(Looking at Winslow Homer's paintings)

Paurotis palms, saw palmettos,
a blue sky pure as thought.
There is beauty, there is light,
and there is death
lurking at the margin of the canvas
in the guise of an alligator
that is deceptively still,
eyeing a roseate spoonbill.

In another late masterwork
a man is stretched out
on the ravaged deck of a small
dismasted fishing boat,
sharks all around, their rolled-up eyes ecstatic.
Off in the far distance,
a tall ship faintly sketched
suggesting salvation is not to be expected.

If those are too dark, take in the next frame:
a Bermuda bungalow
with flowerbed in vivid yellows and reds.
A cloudless watercolour sky.
Though even here you'll note
the little v-shaped tracks
running along the shore
and no bird in sight.

Black

Marie knows
how to mix colours
how to make a black
darker than black

It contrasts with the stars
and the heavenly bodies

It is not political
or racial
not emblematic
of death

It is an earthly
surface smear
that speaks
of what goes
deeper.

III

A Walk Along Lakeshore Drive

You pass lawns prim as golf greens,
boxed flowerbeds with hydrangeas
their inky blue looking as though
it would come off on your hands.

Garden pinwheels hum in the wind.

Eventually you come to the exception:
a dirt yard with two rusted cars,
parts of old dishwashers and AC units,
the netherworld of scrap metal,
grime and oil.

A tethered dog snarls on cue.

If you were to step inside the cabin
you'd find cold linoleum,
a flea market sofa and bed,
an embroidered view of the lake at sunset.
Maybe a rifle in the closet.

What do you find so unsettling?
The hint of violence?
Poverty?

Back in the yard grasshoppers whirr
like broken bits of machinery.
Sunlight thickens on your hand,
honey that's gone hard.

Mayflies

I awake and find them everywhere,
clinging to window screens and car doors,
clustering on the wall of the town's vacant church.
It's hard to tell whether they're alive or dead
until I pinch the wings of one
and feel it squirm, struggling to break free.
When I walk through the dew-soaked playing field,
they rise up around me, a small cloud,
almost biblical. Impossible to forget
their night-time swarms and windshield blinding,
their glistening bits washed up on shore
like flight wreckage, giving off the light
they once gathered in.

Canoe

No need to debate
composites versus aluminum.

Birch bark rules
with its *watap* and spruce resin,
its papery tree rind
negotiating the difficult currents,
coming into still waters, intact.

I steered one once along the Oxtongue River
and it left me speechless.
A feathery wake on the iron water.
A super light resilience
buffering the foreign spirits
gawking on shore.

Old, it smelled of
dried earth, arthritic leaves, animal's breath.

I respected its scarred gunwales,
its nicked ribs of white cedar

its polished thwarts
drinking
the sun.

The Way

Cold sunrise. Visibility one hundred percent.
Leaves on the distant shore
come into perfect focus.

Lao Tzu claimed:
"Without stirring abroad
one can know the whole world."

Now that's a stretch.
Listen, if I hadn't stirred
I wouldn't have crossed Sunbeam Lake
and Flycatcher Bog.

I wouldn't have stood in amazement
at Wolf Howl Pond.

I wouldn't have felt time drip
into my cup
and requested more days
to praise the tree frog,
the water strider.

I wouldn't have heard the red-winged blackbird
warble
before light failed.

"The further one goes" (again, Lao Tzu)
"the less one knows."

I'm good with that
growing more ignorant,
wide-eyed and harmless
among all living things.

Two Trees

Gingko

Oldest species on the planet,
its leaves are lettuce green.

What does it care
whether it's worth a million
more or less?

Oblivious to any accord
signed in Paris
it will grow —
if fortune smiles —
forty feet high or more
evading wires
catching sun

its roots banking
on the nether zones

the mineral deposits

where the wriggly things
make it rich.

Norway Maple

This summer our maple
is too full of itself
spreading imperial shade
that is cool to the skin but death
to the marigolds below.

Their gold and orange want a say
but how can they complain
or mutter? They'll wither in the shadows

which is why I am up here in the boughs
advocating with buzz saw
donning a hat that reads
Blue Jays —

birds
as winged words —

balancing
and cutting back on Norway
to let light in.

Work Poems

Kelly's Tree Service

They arrive late-day,
she's young, willowy
the two guys, brawny
and I assume one of the latter
will put on the harness
but no, she's the one who
grabs the buzz saw as the guys
work the ropes and pulleys
raising her unnervingly high
into the air where
she swings between limbs
severing and trimming
while the two below
collect the fallen branches
and haul them to the chipper
that whirs and grinds and sputters
and when she's done,
she floats back down to earth
and drinks from one of
the bottles of water
I've put out for them.
They're all laughing
as they get back into the truck
and wave,
and after I wave back, I turn
to see the red setting sun,
balancing
between the branches
of the tree.

The Rides

Some days I worked
the mini Ferris wheel,
though I preferred
the carousel with its jovial
pink-tongued elephants
and big-eyed horses. I liked
to see the mothers and fathers
steadying the little ones and
whispering reassuring words
in their ears, and I liked
to watch the older kids,
who were just on the cusp
of adolescence, showing
a modicum of boredom
to let us know that in
another month or so
this would not be for them,
this going around and around
to organ grinder music
while seated on a swan.
Their want would have to
be met by something taller and
steeper, something that put them
upside down, hair, literally,
on end, screaming at a sky
that would never entertain
their pleas as they zoomed down
into the chasm.

Bucky Harris

He had cauliflower ears
and a flattened nose,
gifts from those he'd met
in the ring, both
boxing and
wrestling. He'd fought
on Juno Beach
and all he cared to tell me
was how sick he'd been
on the landing craft, how fast
his feet carried him
over sand, and now
he was showing me
how to work the levers
on the Ferris wheel,
do a simple fix
on the gears,
and by example
how to avoid fights
on the midway
without losing self-
respect. In the
the bar at night
where we drank
I offered him a joint,
and he looked at me
askance. I think
of how there are

few men left
of his generation,
men who spoke
infrequently, and
meant it
when they did.

United Tire Corp.

I have learned
how to roll tires
across the floor
and into the hands of
Jimmy Picard, who stacks
them on cold metal racks
that sit under the hands
of the company clock.
And the clock
is on a wall
under a filthy window
that lets in
just enough light
to make out
the suffocating motes
of dust and debris,
without destroying
the dramatic effect
of that fiery lit Vulcan
who hammers shut
the metal mould
and pours in the black.

Meat Packing

Guard this tool
with your life,
its sharp little prong
is what you'll need
to get clogged meat
out of the chopper
and remember
to turn off the power
before going in:
we don't want your finger
ending up
in a package of dogs,
believe me it's happened.
Wear layers —
it's cold at 8 a.m.
but heats up like a steam-bath
once the engines get revving
and don't bother speaking
to whoever is next to you,
no one can hear.
Wear shoes that grip,
the floor gets slippery
with animal fat
and before leaving
don't forget to punch out,
don't slam the door
when you get home,

don't sulk
at the kitchen table,
soak yourself
in something strong
the smell of this place
clings to the skin.

Cow

> "When the ancient Dawns rose,
> the Great Syllable was born
> in the footprint of the Cow."
> —*Rigveda*

I can believe it,
having watched
a white Brahman
garlanded with cream
and crimson flowers
walk through the streets
of Madras.
I recall thinking,
Why shouldn't an animal
rhythmically rocking
from hoof to hollowed hoof,
leaving joyful impressions
in the damp earth
while swaying her tail
like a metronome,
be considered
the mother of all sound?
So composed, so unlikely
to scare, shedding
majestic calm,
her eyes, the rich brown
of Indian coffee.
Who would deny
such a creature?
Not the women I heard
in flame-coloured saris
slapping their laundry
against the rocks
of the Adyar river

singing their hymns
in unison, and not
the earthen-skinned man
who popped up next to me,
a bulging snake
wrapped around his neck
chanting his
blessings.
No, this is not Elsie,
or Bessie,
I told myself,
as I watched her halt
at the end of the street
and tilt her wreathed head
toward the potter's stall
listening
for the deep hum
of his wheel.

Tailor

He unravels a bolt of cloth
urging you to feel
the texture of worsted

to marvel
at houndstooth, herringbone,
birdseye and sharkskin, from the mills

of Quebec, from jobbers in Manhattan,
from Leeds and the Hebrides
who send us the solid Harris tweed.

He would like you to say the names:
mohair, flannel, nap, and twill,
pinstripe, chalk stripe, hopsack, check.

He wants you to know the origin of seersucker
from the Persian *shir shakar*, "milk and sugar."
And from the goats of the Gobi the truest cashmere.

He probes: cuffs or no cuffs,
belt or no belt, pleats or no pleats?
How wide the lapel?

His measuring tape is draped
like a thin prayer shawl about his neck
in that shop where God has grown personal

and small, crouched inside a pitted thimble.
He relies on vision and hands
to match facings, linings, to tack the seams,

then cut, resew, close the gap
between pattern and flesh, between ideal and real,
with the mirror as your witness

524 Glengarry

Don't spend time
recalling that street
of maples and lilacs.
Let someone else
remember the families
who once gathered
on the summer porches
and let him curse
whoever it was
that worked the numbers
so they could demolish
the ancient frames
along with the flower beds
and rose trellis,
the sandbox and swing.
You're done with mourning.
The copper-plated roof
of that new house
shines with amnesia.
The skylight sees
clear through into air,
the address anywhere.

Survey

All torn down, Sloan's Tavern, Dave's Grill,
Rosie's Ice Cream Parlour. The destroyed
towns of Ontario. The ripped up
public piers of Jackson's Point and Beaverton,
carted to the hammer mill.
The scale of degradation visible.
Take our old dirt road, paved, blackened.
Stuttering white hyphens. Holes
in the landscape I can measure.
The soft wooden floor of Burroughs' Hardware,
its yellow blinds and antique light.
All torn down. Night after night,
walking Lakeshore Drive,
smelling lilacs and thinking of her.
I knew the name of every creek.

An Inherited Garden

I wonder if anyone before me stood here
smelling the garden bed's cat piss
or held the leaf of this spirea to the sun
examining its tiny veins.
Did someone else happen to rub mint
between his thumb and fingers
or drop basil leaves into a plastic pail
and hum all the way to the kitchen?
Who else peered through the splintered fence
imagining the bizarre life of his neighbours?
God of the living bough,
did anyone else rest in the shade of this elm
holding a buttercup under his chin
or pick petals to see if someone loved him?

Hits of the 50s

Heartbreak Hotel comes over our radio
and I sing along mimicking "The King."
Afterward, I am stuck on the phrase
"found a new place to dwell."
The last word sounds so biblical.

I dwell with my family in a small rented bungalow
with a second-hand TV. Father works from sun-up to evening.
Mother takes in sewing, keeps up with Th*e Secret Storm,*
The Edge of Night. Soap operas take her
from the opera of our lives.

The house across the street has all its rooms
torn into view: furniture gone, floors ripped up,
wires dangling like cold spaghetti.
This is the new world
and the air downtown is difficult to breathe.

Each night, under the glare of streetlamps,
June bugs scrape and migrate like fellow refugees
along the bleached pavement
while I lie in bed with the window open
smelling lilacs from the neighbour's yard.

I'm listening to a car radio play *The Poor People of Paris.*
The music stops and it grows dark.
It's a darkness I've never known before,
a darkness
without any stars.

Mrs. Ono's Guesthouse

(For Marie)

Kyoto. Decades back. She had no vacancy
but found a closet-like space for us
in the rear of her courtyard. Green tea,

tatami, a cold-water faucet we shared
with two girls from Oz. Short-haired travellers,
their "no worries" take on things

had buoyed them over three continents.
Streets with no names, no numbers,
how did we locate that talked-about sushi house

run by a young husband and wife —
our industrious doubles — laughing
as they cut cold fish?

Our late-night walks along the Kamogawa River
where lovers sat holding hands.
Lamps, lanterns, shot glasses of light

wavering on the raven-winged water.
Do we search the face of the other
to find who we are? Is the connection only imagined?

Mrs. Ono regarded me with suspicion,
while for you she showed the deepest concern.
Worrying over your cough on the morning we left,

she gave you a handful of lozenges
before tying two miniature bells to your knapsack.
"For good luck," she said. "For the long road."

Skunk

Returning to bed
after a late-night piss
I open the blinds and am startled to see
the white, luxurious stripe
of the skunk.

It's early March and she's risen
from her winter torpor
with nocturnal business of her own,
digging in the damp turf,
frantic for food.

She waddles along the bed
of the privet hedge I planted decades back
and still flourishing
while loved ones since have passed,
their bones freed from memory.

And now she stops in her tracks
to lift her wedge-head
and sniff at the cold night air.
Moonlight catches the flash
of her alien, amber eyes.

Where does she live? Under
our weathered deck,
beneath the side door's
crumbling step
that I never got around to fixing?

Once I stumbled upon her at dusk
as I went to wind up the garden hose.
We stared at each other,
then each of us
took off in opposite directions.

Her world is sparse and unspeaking,
while mine is flooded with words — the din
of misapprehension.
But not now.
Not at this late hour.

Concession Road A

I'm not too old to walk it
to go on as far as it goes
since it's mostly paved
curving only by the cornfield
where it brings on the crows
and where the breeze off the lake
combs the stalks
and straightens out again
then gradually narrows
turning from asphalt
to gravel and dust
with that stencilled sign
Use At Your Own Risk
though what risk can there be
walking at such a pace
away from everything
except the bulging black eyes
of the cows that follow me
with complete indifference
as I make my way
toward the brooding
congregation of trees.

Acknowledgements

Thanks to the editors of the following journals, where several of these poems first appeared: The *Antigonish Review, Canadian Literature, The Dalhousie Review, The Ekphrastic Review, Grain, Literary Review of Canada, Peripheries, Harvard University (US), Prairie Fire, Queen's Quarterly, Raritan (US), Southern Poetry Review (US), Stand (UK).*

I want to thank Michael Mirolla for his support. My writing group (Judy, Dorothy, the two Davids, Lynn, Rita, Tannaz, Carol, Clare, and Bob) gave essential feedback on several of the poems. Also, Shel Krakofsky, David Penhale, and Carol Lipszyc.

And the Muse — Marie.

About the Author

Kenneth Sherman has published ten books of poetry, including the long poems *Words for Elephant Man* and *Black River*. He has also published three books of prose. His memoir, *Wait Time*, was nominated for the 2017 RBC/Taylor nonfiction prize. He has twice won the Canadian Jewish book award, once for his poetry collection, *Jackson's Point*, and once for his essay collection, *What the Furies Bring*. He resides in Toronto where he conducts poetry workshops.

Also by Kenneth Sherman

Poetry

Snake Music
The Cost of Living
Words for Elephant Man
Black Flamingo
Relations: An Anthology of Family Poems (editor)
The Book of Salt
Jackson's Point
Open to Currents
Clusters
The Well
Black River
Jogging with the Great Ray Charles

Prose

Void and Voice: Essays on Historical and Literary Currents
What the Furies Bring
Wait Time: A Memoir of Cancer

MIX
Paper
FSC® C100212
FSC
www.fsc.org

Printed by Imprimerie Gauvin
Gatineau, Québec